Dedicated to my students,
who have been a source of joy and inspiration.

Revised for reprint 1991
Reformatted 1994
Reprinted 1996

ISBN 0-9619229-3-1

Printed in U.S.A.

Table of Contents

Speed Tailoring

Speed tailoring is a new method of tailoring which allows us to achieve a very professional look in a very short period of time. This is possible because of new methods of sewing and trimming, the reduction of handwork, a minimum of marking, and the use of new materials such as fusible interfacing.

The purpose of this book is to help the student or home sewer construct a woman's lined jacket or blazer using the fastest and most effective speed tailoring techniques.

Pattern Selection and Adjustment

In order to take advantage of as many techniques as possible, choose a pattern with a full lining, set-in sleeves, and set-in collar. Sleeve vents and center back vents are optional. Pocket style is a matter of personal preference.

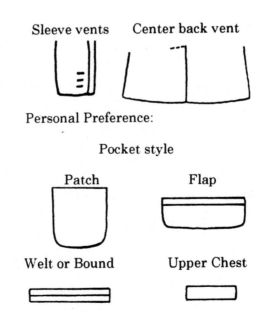

Recommended Style

Since it is easier to adjust the waist, bust, and hip areas than the shoulders, buying a pattern to fit your shoulders is the first step toward a good fit. This is difficult because pattern companies do not give shoulder measurements on the pattern covers.

Arrive at the best size by averaging your ready-to-wear size and your previous pattern size. Take into account the proportion of your shoulders in relation to your bust and hips. If your shoulders are narrow, buy a size smaller than the size you would get to fit your bust and hips. If your shoulders are wide and you feel you always need more room in that area, you may want a size larger than the one you usually buy.

If you already have the pattern and need to adjust the shoulders, take the measurement from a jacket you own, or try some jackets on in a store and take the measurement from one that fits in the shoulders. A coat will be 1 to 2" wider in the shoulders than a jacket.

If you are unsure what length to make your jacket, a general rule is to start at the widest part of the hips and lengthen or shorten according to personal taste. Take this measurement from the center back neck seam to the hem. The best way to decide is to measure a jacket you own, or try some on to determine what length is becoming to you.

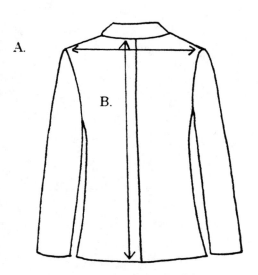

A. Shoulder width
B. Jacket length

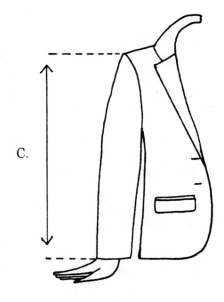

C. Sleeve length

Next, adjust the length of the sleeves. The proper length for sleeves is determined by standing with your arms at your sides and by bending your hands up at the wrists. The sleeves should come to the crease where the wrists bend. Measure from the shoulder to the crease with the arms straight. If you are measuring a completed jacket, measure from the shoulder seam to the hem of the sleeve.

After adjustments for length have been made, measure the pattern around and take in or let out as needed in the bust, waist, and hip areas. Remember, you must have extra room for ease of movement. The bust and hip areas should have at least 3" extra as an average. The amount of ease is different depending on the pattern style, fabric, and personal preference. When in doubt, add a little extra.

It is very rare to find an underarm bust dart on a jacket pattern, and if you wear a C cup or larger, you will probably need to add one. Without a side dart, curved diagonal lines form from the lower waist up to the bust area. To add a bust dart:

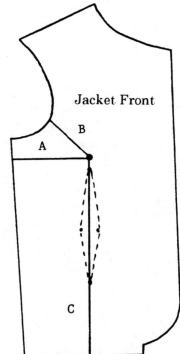

Jacket Front

1. Put a dot on the pattern at the point of the bust.
2. Draw a new dart line horizontally from the sideseam to the point. (Line A)
3. Draw another line diagonally from the armhole to the point. (Line B)
4. Draw a line from the point vertically to the jacket bottom. (Line C)

5. Slash line A from the side-seam to the bust point, but not through it.

6. Starting at the bottom of the pattern piece, slash up line C, through the bust point, and to the armhole but not through it, on line B.

7. Spread the pattern apart by pulling over and down on the section with the new dart line.
Spread: 1/2" for C cup
             3/4 - 1" for D cup
              1 - 2" for larger than D
This pulling automatically spreads the new dart apart.

8. Slash and lengthen the front section.

9. Draw in the new dart and redraw the lines of the vertical waist dart, blending the lines in.

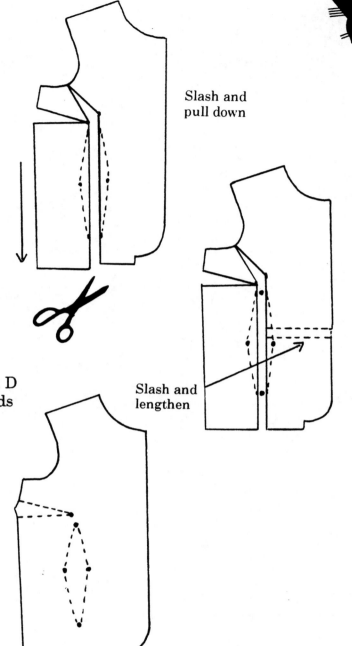

Slash and pull down

Slash and lengthen

      The first time you do this, it will be experimental, so you may want to make a muslin fitting shell. After you find how much to spread the pattern for your figure, you can routinely add that sized dart to every pattern needing one.
      Make any other adjustments to the pattern according to prior knowledge of your own fitting problems. Don't forget to alter all lining pieces too.

Fabric Selection

Wool is the ultimate fabric to tailor because it will ease beautifully, is durable, and will press well. Use 100% wool or blends of polyester and wool or nylon and wool for your first choice. Tweed is the easiest and most forgiving fabric in this category. Solid colors and smoother finished fabrics like flannel and gabardine are more difficult because details show.

For medium weight garments, silk is excellent. Some polyester suitings are also appropriate, as well as blends of silk and polyester. Linen and ramie make versatile jackets, but they can wrinkle. Corduroy, in the medium weight category, is the most difficult fabric to tailor because it does not ease and is hard to press.

Fusible interfacing cannot be fused to velvet because it cannot be pressed conventionally. However, some 100% cotton velveteens can be pressed, and I have used them successfully.

Summer jackets can be made of poplin, seersucker, and other light weight fabrics.

Your fabric *MUST BE PRESHRUNK* even if the label says it has been preshrunk or sponged, as is the case with some wool. Wool or wool blends can be steamed at the drycleaner's, as should any unwashable fabric. Washable fabrics can be preschrunk by washing and drying them according to the instructions on their care labels.

Selection of lining is very much up to personal taste. Silk is the most elegant lining for wool because it is a natural fiber, but it is expensive. Polyester makes a very durable and attractive lining and is more reasonably priced. Rayon is not as durable and is sometimes more likely to wrinkle, but is breathes better than polyester. Some of the designer or signature linings can give your garment a finished look. Lining *MUST BE PRESHRUNK* according to its care label.

Findings

Even though the pattern will call for less, you will need two yards of interfacing for a jacket and three yards for a coat. The weight of interfacing is determined by the type of outer fabric you use.

For jackets in light to medium weight fabrics like tweed, worsted, gabardine, corduroy, suit weight sild, linen, velveteen, and cotton, use a suit weight fusible weft insertion interfacing.

For heavy fabric (or any fabric you are using for a coat), I recommend a fusible horsehair canvas.

If you are not sure which weight to use, buy a small amount of several interfacings and do some test samples with your fabric. This will help you determine which gives body to the fabric without changing the general characteristics of the fabric. If you are new to tailoring, a general rule is to use the weft insertion in jackets and the fusible horsehair in coats.

You will need a pair of medium weight shoulder pads. Shoulder pads are a necessity in every tailored jacket because they form the basis for the drape of the whole garment. Without them, diagonal lines will pull from the shoulders to the bust. Refer to the "Shoulder Pad Application" chapter for a description of proper shoulder pads.

Purchase a set of sleeve heads or cut your own from a spongy interfacing like Thermolam or Pellon Fleece Make them 12" by 1 1/2".

Look through your scrap box to find some leftover seam tape that is close in color to your fabric. You will need twelve inches or two, six-inch pieces to stabilize the shoulder seams. If you don't have any scraps, purchase a package of twill tape.

Two optional sewing aides are tailor's chalk for marking and beeswax for hand sewing.

Layout, Cutting, and Marking

Lay the pattern out according to the pattern directions. Begin now to develop a policy of always folding the right side of the fabric to the inside. This will minimize confusion during construction and will make marking easier. Treat the lining in the same manner.

If your pattern has sleeve vents that are cut unevenly, as for mitered corners, fill in the missing areas. Both extensions should be the same size, usually 1" in width and whatever length the pattern designates.

Fill in the missing areas:

Now cut the pattern out. Instead of cutting around the notches, cut the notches off. As you do this, make a 1/4" clip into the seam allowance to mark their position. Clip the position of all dots in the same manner.

Clip the notches   Clip the dots

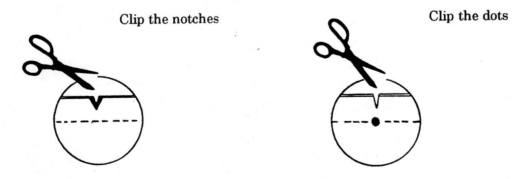

Next, mark the darts in whichever way you find easiest, whether it be with pins, chalk, or tailor tacks. This is all the marking to be done at this time.

Cutting the Interfacing

When cutting the interfacing, *DO NOT USE THE INTERFACING PIECES FROM THE PATTERN*. Instead, use the pattern pieces themselves, following the grainlines, and trim away 5/8" all around. The interfacing should come up to the seamlines but not into them. From the scraps of interfacing, cut several strips, as wide as the hem (usually 1 1/2" or 1 1/4""), and any length. These will be used to reinforce the jacket and sleeve hems. Cut the interfacing on the same grain as the pattern pieces.

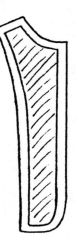

Front Facing:
Cut 4 pieces (2 sets),
and trim away 5/8" all
around.

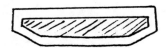

Upper Collar:
Cut 1 piece and trim.

Chest pocket:
Cut 1 piece and trim.

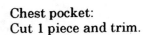

Under Collar:
Cut 2 pieces (1 set),
and trim.

Patch and Flap
pockets:
Cut 1 set but
DO NOT TRIM.

Back Neck Facing:
Cut 1 piece and trim.

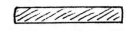

Strips for hems.

*Note: from now on, the wrong side of the fabric will be dotted and the interfacing will be scored diagonally.

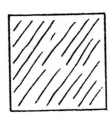

Wrong Side   Interfacing

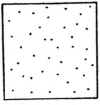

Fusing the Interfacing

Before fusing the interfacing pieces, it is necessary to understand the importance of pressing in the whole tailoring process. In traditional tailoring, pad stitching is used to attach the interfacing and to shape jacket parts. In speed tailoring, the iron is used to perform both these functions.

The iron really has three uses, ironing, steaming, and pressing, and each is quite distinct. Ironing is the most common use and its purpose is to remove wrinkles from entire garments or from large areas of garments. It can be done with a dry iron or with steam. A minimum of pressure is used while sliding the iron back and forth.

Steaming is done by holding the iron away from the fabric while allowing the steam to penetrate it. It is used to ease or shrink fabric in areas like the sleeve cap. Steaming can also be used to remove wrinkles from napped fabrics or to restore the nap if it has been flattened. A shot-of-steam iron works well for steaming because the flow of steam can be regulated.

Ironing

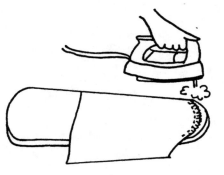

Steaming

Pressing is the process used most in tailoring and is done by applying heat, moisture, and pressure to small areas of the garment at a time. It is used for fusing interfacing, molding, shaping, and permanently setting parts of the garment into place. The iron stays in one place instead of moving back and forth. Because the iron is put directly on the fabric and force is applied, always use a press cloth unless you have tested your fabric carefully beforehand.

Always allow garments and garment parts to cool in the position in which they were pressed. The principle here is similar to the one used in electric rollers for hair. By using heat, moisture, and pressure, and allowing the pressed area to become cool and dry, the press will "set."

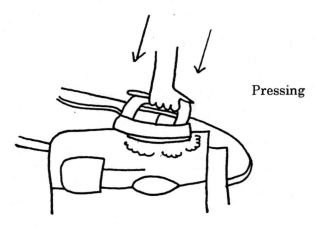

Pressing

Armed with this information, you can now proceed to fuse the interfacing. Follow the manufacturer's instructions, remembering to press straight down. After fusing one area, lift the iron and go to another area instead of sliding it. Lie the pieces on a flat surface to cool.

If bubbles appear, press again until they are gone. If the interfacing starts to come off or bubble during construction of the garment, this means you haven't fused it enough. Just reapply the iron where needed. Sometimes the interfacing will form a ridge on the Jacket Fronts. If this happens on your garment, apply some heat and steam to the edge of the interfacing and peel it back. Trim the edge with a pinking shears and fuse it again. This should help the edge blend in.

Finally, take the interfacing strips and fuse them along the bottom of the jacket and sleeves. Go up to the hemlines but not into them. You may piece these strips.

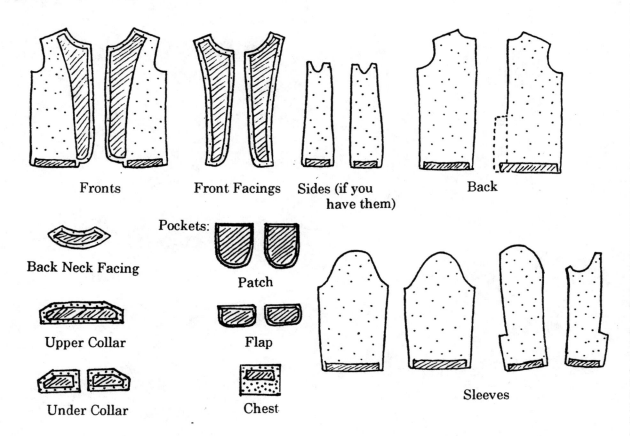

Fronts Front Facings Sides (if you have them) Back

Back Neck Facing

Pockets: Patch

Upper Collar Flap

Under Collar Chest

Sleeves

Bound Buttonholes

If you want bound buttonholes on your garment, now is the time to apply them. *Note: bound buttonholes are simply small bound pockets. Assuming you are using 3/4" or 7/8" buttons, following are directions for one inch buttonholes.

1. Cut a strip of fabric 1" x 8" and fuse interfacing to the entire wrong side of the strip.

2. Fold the strip in half lengthwise, wrong sides together, and press it flat. Stitch 1/8" from the folded edge.

3. Cut the strip into four 2" pieces. These will be the welts or lips for the buttonholes.

4. On the garment Front, sew a ladder to mark the location of the buttonholes.

5. With the folded edges away from the center of the buttonhole, match the stitching lines of the welts with the stitching lines of the buttonholes. There will be 1/2" extra on each end. Sew one welt at a time, checking to see if the stitching lines up on the wrong side.

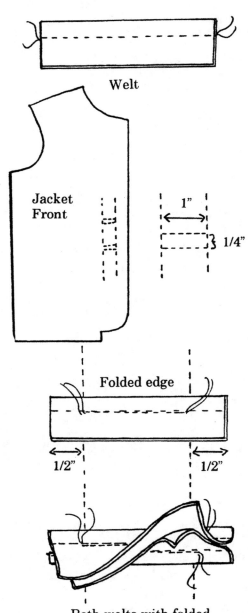

13

6. Go to the wrong side and slash through the middle of the boxes and diagonally out to the corners.

7. Turn the welts and press.

8. Sew back and forth over the triangles by folding the outer fabric back.

Slash

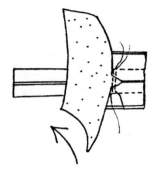

Sew over the triangles

The Front Facing must be sewn to the jacket before the buttonholes can be completed, so for now, you are done with them. Proceed with the next steps of construction and return to this page when instructed.

The Facing

1. Sew two oblong boxes, 1" x 1/4", on the facing at the buttonhole locations. Use smaller than normal stitches.

1. Sew the boxes

2. Slash the boxes just as you slashed the buttonholes.

2. Slash

3. Slipstitch the facing to the stitching lines of the buttonhole welts, turning the Facing under as you go. Take small stitches and try to hide them in the seam. Press.

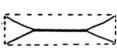

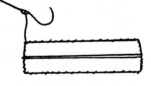

3. Turn under and tack to the welts

14

Backstitching

Backstitching is a very important part of the construction of any garment. Backstitching is used to reinforce the seams so they won't unravel. The absence of backstitching is evident in many ready-to-wear garments where the seams and darts frequently rip open before the first wearing.

In the past, many of us were taught to backstitch right at the beginning and at the end of each seam. This has been proven ineffective because when the seams are trimmed, the backstitching is trimmed off too.

Instead, stitch in 5/8" and backstitch there. Then the backstitching will remain after the trimming is done. At the end of the row of stitching, stop 5/8" from the edge, backstitch, and finish the seam.

Incorrect:
Backstitching is trimmed off.

Correct:
Backstitching remains.

Darts

Stitch the darts and be sure to backstitch at the points or tie the threads. Trim the darts to 1/4" from the seam and to 1 1/2" from the points. Press the darts open and the points toward the center of the garment.

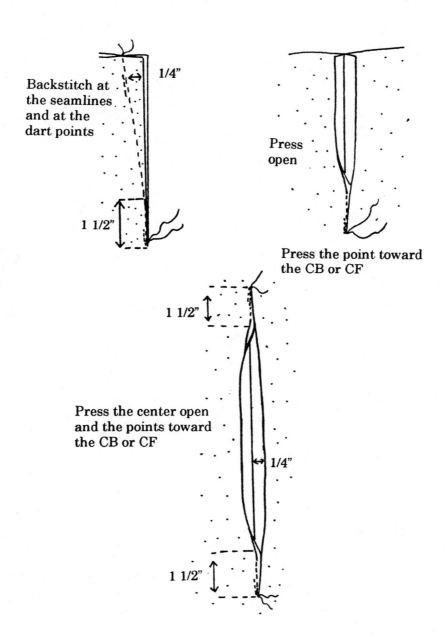

Backstitch at the seamlines and at the dart points

1/4"

1 1/2"

Press open

Press the point toward the CB or CF

Press the center open and the points toward the CB or CF

1 1/2"

1/4"

1 1/2"

Upper Chest Pocket

Now, apply the upper chest pocket if your pattern has one. If you are not going to wear a handkerchief in the pocket, I recommend you make it fake. This is because on women, the bust can cause the pocket to gap open. Making a fake pocket is easy:

1. Fold the welt in half, right sides together, and stitch the sides.

2. Trim the seams to 1/4".

3. Turn and press.

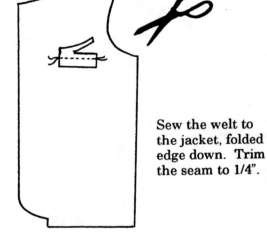

Sew the welt to the jacket, folded edge down. Trim the seam to 1/4".

4. Sew the welt to the jacket, folded edge down.

5. Trim the seam to 1/4".

6. Fold the welt up and press.

7. Topstitch close to the edge on each side.

Fold the welt up and topstitch.

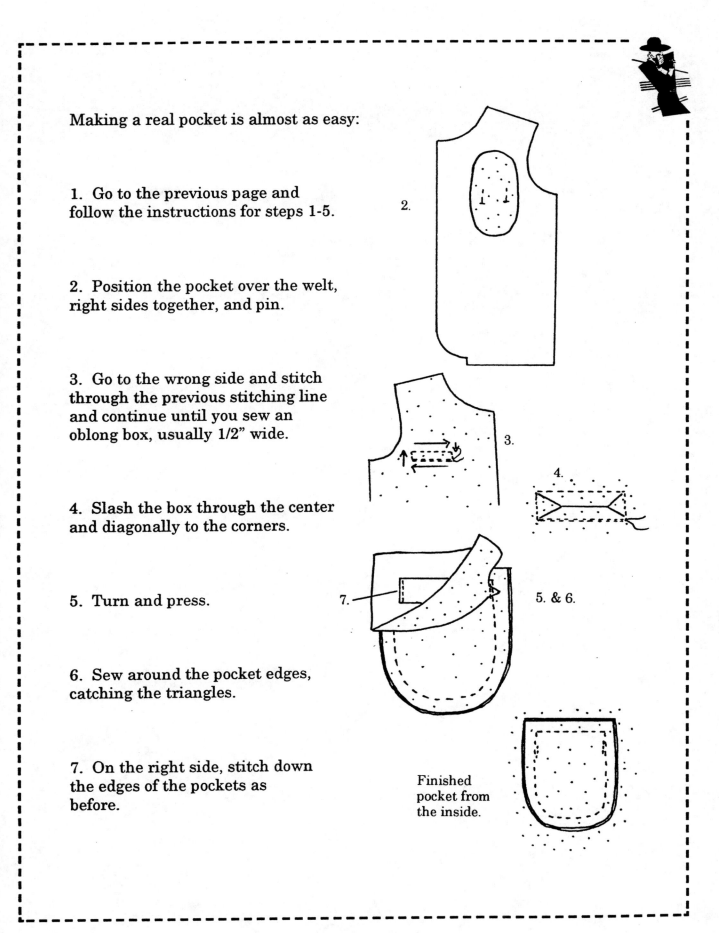

Making a real pocket is almost as easy:

1. Go to the previous page and follow the instructions for steps 1-5.

2. Position the pocket over the welt, right sides together, and pin.

3. Go to the wrong side and stitch through the previous stitching line and continue until you sew an oblong box, usually 1/2" wide.

4. Slash the box through the center and diagonally to the corners.

5. Turn and press.

6. Sew around the pocket edges, catching the triangles.

7. On the right side, stitch down the edges of the pockets as before.

Finished pocket from the inside.

Sideseams

Sew the center back seam and the sideseams from the bottom up. Press them open. If you have a CB (center back) vent, baste it closed and press.

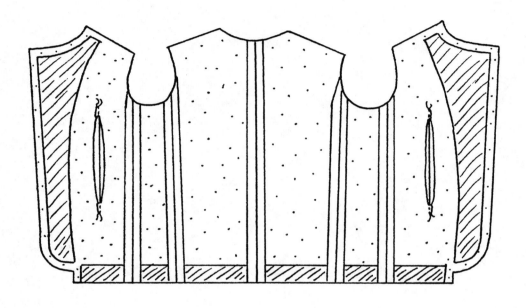

Baste the vent closed, clip the seam so the vent can be pressed to the right.

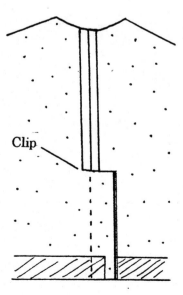

Clip

Shoulder Seams

Keep the shoulder seams firm and free from stretching by sewing a piece of tape right into the seams. Use twill tape or a piece of seam tape which is nearly the same color as your fabric. Do not use bias tape because it stretches. After sewing, press the seams firmly so they will lie open.

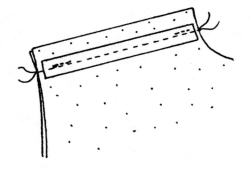

Sew tape into the seam

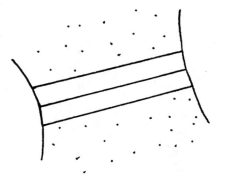

Press open

Staystitching

We do not staystitch extensively on the garment because it is constructed so quickly. The pieces are handled so little, there is little time for stretching. Staystitch only the neck opening all around at 1/2". Use a normal stitch length and sew from the CB to the front on one side and then the other.

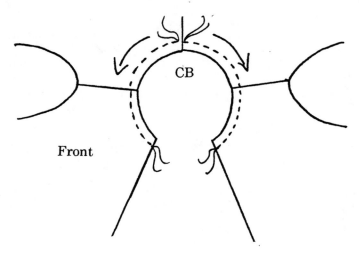

Collar Application

This method of collar application, similar to the method of collar application in blouses, is probably the most important speed tailoring procedure. It drastically reduces the time spent in traditional collar application methods and it produces a perfect collar and lapels with no bulges, puckers, or gaps.

1. Sew the center back seam of the Under Collar and press it open.

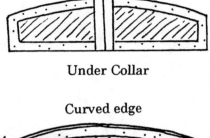

Under Collar

2. Pin the Upper Collar to the Under Collar, right sides together. Match the center backs and the points of the corners. You will be pinning the straight edge, not the curved edge. The Upper Collar may be bigger than the Under Collar. This extra fabric allows the Upper Collar to roll smoothly over the Under Collar.

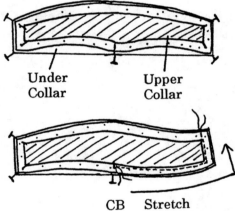

Curved edge

Under Collar   Upper Collar

CB   Stretch

3. Sew the outer edge and the sides of the collar together, stretching as you sew to ease in the Upper Collar. This will make the Upper Collar curl over the Under Collar naturally. To make the collar symmetrical, sew from the CB out and around in one direction and then the other. Make a diagonal stitch over each corner This helps make the corners square when turned right side out.

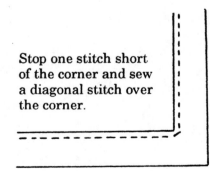

Stop one stitch short of the corner and sew a diagonal stitch over the corner.

4. Trim the collar seams to 1/4" all around and diagonally over the corners. The seams are not graded because this would make it harder to press them flat.

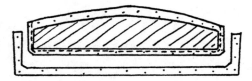

Trim seams to 1/4" all around.

5. Turn the collar right sides out and press well on the Under Collar side. This avoids scorching the Upper Collar. Press from the center out toward the points in a circular motion. Pressing from the underside will also help the Upper Collar curl back over the Under Collar.

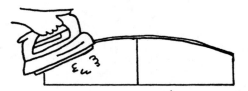

Press on the Under Collar side.

6. Match up the raw edges of the Upper and Under Collar if they are uneven. Pin the collar to the jacket matching the center back seams and extending the collar edges to the clips in the Jacket Fronts.

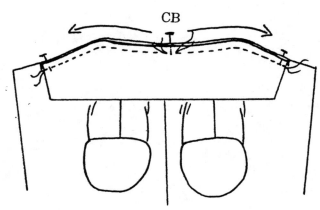

7. Baste the collar in place, but do not trim the seams. Sew from the CB out to each side . This keeps the collar symmetrical.

Sew from the CB out in each direction.

Facing and Lapel Application

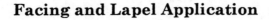

1. Sew the Back Neck Facing to the Front Facing pieces and press the seams open.

2. Pin the Facing to the jacket, right over the collar. Sew from the CB out and down on each side. Make a diagonal stitch over each corner. If the Facing lapels are larger than the jacket lapels, stretch the two as you sew to ease in the fullness. This will make the lapels fold back automatically when they are turned and pressed. Sew around the bottom curves up to 1" from the edges.

Back Neck Facing

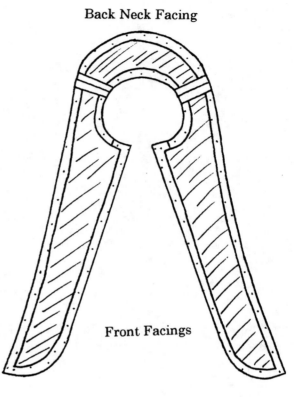

Front Facings

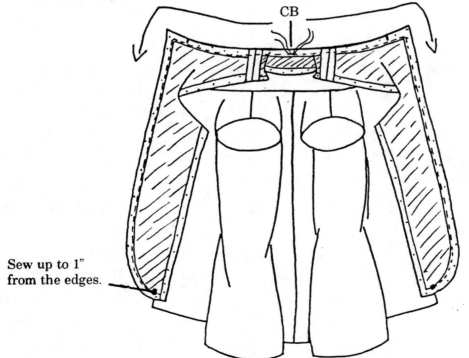

CB

Sew up to 1" from the edges.

3. Trim the entire seam through all thicknesses to 1/4", and diagonally over the corners. Use pinking shears on the curves. Do not grade the seams.

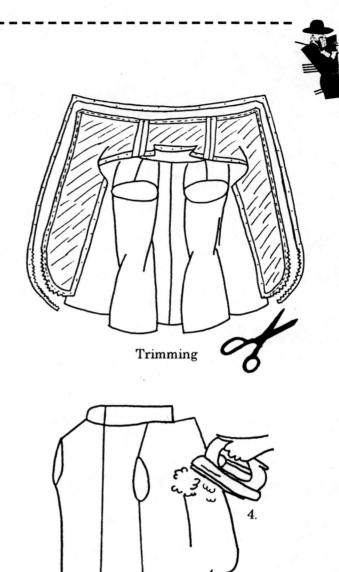

Trimming

4. Turn and press. Press the lapels on the underside. Press halfway down the Jacket Front.

5. Then turn the jacket over and press the botton curved edge on the inside. Press halfway up the Jacket Front.

The most important parts of the jacket are the collar and lapels. When people look at us, they look at our faces first, and then at our collar and lapels. Because of this, press these most visible parts on the underside to avoid the risk of scorching.

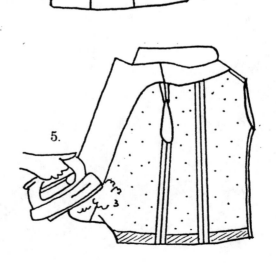

The Jacket Hem

Now press the hem up and attach it with a whip stitch or catch stitch. Make the stitches loose so they don't show on the outside. The two stitches are illustrated below. To keep the thread from tangling, draw it through beeswax before sewing.

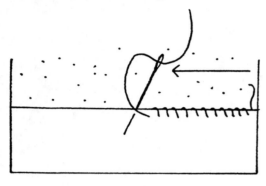

Whip Stitch

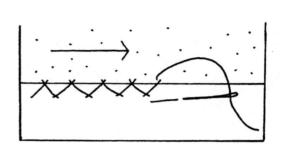

Catch Stitch

For a CB vent, tack as illustrated, after removing vent basting.

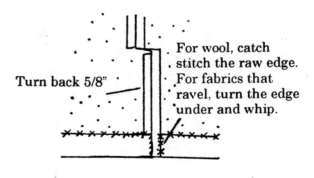

Turn back 5/8"

For wool, catch stitch the raw edge. For fabrics that ravel, turn the edge under and whip.

On the outside, topstitch diagonally over the top of the vent.

Topstitch the vent on the outside.

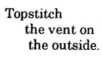

*Note: if you made bound buttonholes, return to page 14 and tack them to the Facing.

Pocket Application

We have waited for pocket application until the Facings and hem are done for two reasons. First, inaccuracies in sewing the Facings and hem would make the pockets uneven. Secondly, since the jacket shell can now be tried on, you can experiment with pocket location, moving them to see where they are most flattering.

To do this, trace the pocket pattern twice, minus seam allowances. Pin the tissue pockets to the jacket at the recommended positions. Then move them in, out, up, or down, to see where they look best on your body (Fig. A)..

If your jacket has patch pockets, and you want flap pockets, use the lower third of the patch pocket to make a flap pattern (Fig. B). The flaps are placed on the jacket where the top of the patch pockets would have been.

If your pattern has patch or flap pockets and you want bound pockets, simply make welts and place them where the top of the patch or flap pockets would have been.

Fig. A
Move the pocket around
to determine the
best position.
Dotted lines
show position
of flap and
bound
pockets.

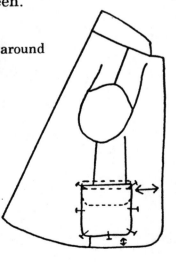

Fig. B

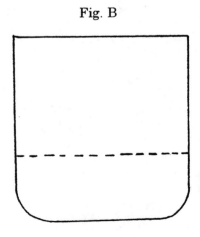

Patch Pockets

1. Sew the lining to the pocket, right sides together.

2. Bring the bottom of the lining down to meet the bottom of the pocket and pin it all around. The seam goes down but do not press it. Leave a 2" opening at the bottom.

3. Now sew from the opening around and up. Turn to the other side and sew from the other end of the opening around and up.

4. Trim the straight part of the sides to 1/4" and use pinking shears to trim to 1/4" around the curved corners. Do not trim the opening.

5. Turn the pocket right side out and press. The opening will be stitched together when we attach the pocket to the jacket with topstitching.

6. After positioning the pockets on the jacket, topstitch them in place using whatever topstitching width you have chosen. To reinforce the corners, start with 1/2' of the smallest zig-zag, stitch around, and finish with the 1/2" of zig-zag.

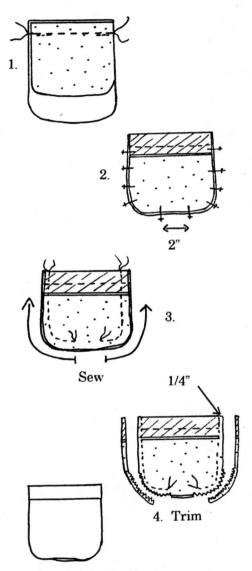

1.

2.

2"

3.

Sew

1/4"

4. Trim

5. Pocket back showing opening

6. Topstitched pocket

Bound Pockets

Bound pockets are merely large bound buttonholes with facings and pockets attached inside.

1. Cut 4 strips of fabric 2" by the length of the pockets plus 2" (for 5" pockets, the strips would be 2" x 7"). Fuse interfacing to the entire wrong side of the strips.

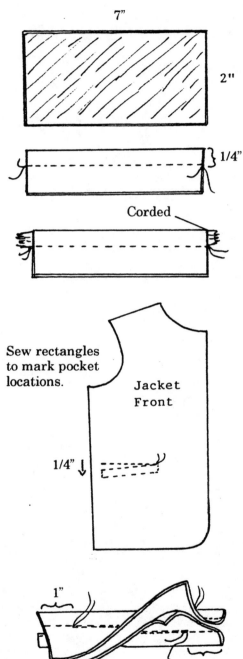

2. Fold the strips in half lengthwise, wrong sides together, and stitch 1/4" from the folded edge. You can also put 1/4" cording in if desired. These will be the welts for the pockets.

3. Sew rectangles on your garment at the pocket locations. Make them 1/2" x the length of the pockets.

*Note: instead of positioning the pockets straight across, you can lower the outside points 1/4". This makes a diagonal line which is more slimming on the body.

4. Center the stitching line of the welts over the stitching lines of the rectangles with folded edges of the welts away from the center of the rectangles. Sew using a smaller than normal stitch length.

You may want to hand baste them first. There will be 1" extra on each end of the welts.

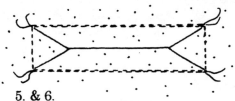

5. & 6.
Check stitching lines and slash.

5. Check on the inside of the garment to see if the stitching lines of the welts match the stitching lines of the rectangles. If not, rip and correct.

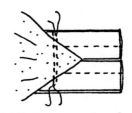

7. Sew over triangles.

6. Slash straight across the center of the pocket rectangles and diagonally out to the corners. Stop 1/2" from the ends and slash all the way to the corners.

7. Turn the welts and sew down the triangles.

8. Sew the pockets to the bottom welts, right sides together.

9. Cut two facing pieces, 2" x the length of the pocket plus 2" (for 5" pockets they would be 2" x 7").

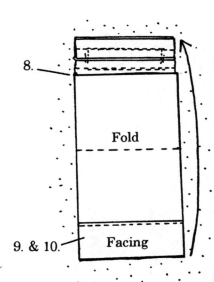

8.

Fold

Facing

9. & 10.

10. Position the facing pieces on the pockets so when the pockets are folded up, the facings will be behind the pocket openings. Sew them to the pockets.

11. Fold the pockets up and stitch the tops to the raw edges of the welts. Stitch the sides.

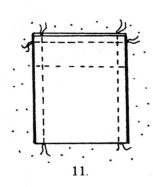

11.

Flap Pockets

A flap pocket is a combination of a bound pocket and the bottom part of a patch pocket. These instructions will be very different, but much easier and more professional than the ones in the pattern.

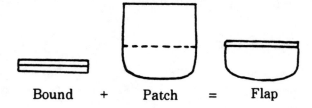

Bound + Patch = Flap

1. Sew the lining to the flaps, right sides together. The flaps will be more symmetrical if you sew from the center out in each direction.

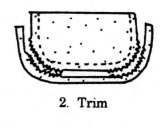

1. Sew

2. Trim the edges to 1/4" on the straight and with the pinking shears on the curves.

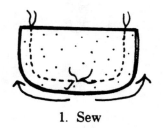

2. Trim

3. Turn and press. Topstitch if desired.

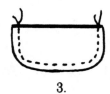

3.

4. Go to the previous instructions for bound pockets and make two bound pockets on your jacket. Do not angle the pockets unless your pattern has angled flaps, or the grain will be off. Make the openings the same length as the flaps but do not sew the inside pockets to the welts yet.

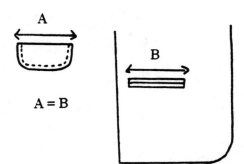

A

B

A = B

5. Take the flaps and insert them into the welts.

6. On the inside, sew the flaps to the raw edges of the upper welts.

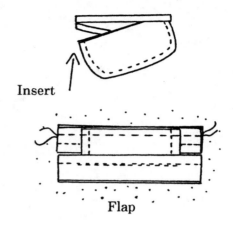

Insert

Flap

7. Sew the pockets to the lower welts, right sides together.

8. Fold the pockets up and sew them to the raw edges of the upper welts.

9. Sew the sides of the pockets. Turn to the right side of the jacket, and using a press cloth, press the pockets over a ham to simulate the curves of the body. Allow the pockets to cool in this position before proceeding.

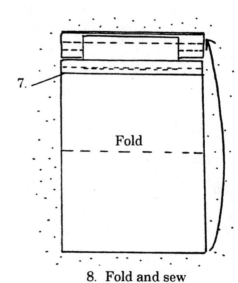

7.

Fold

8. Fold and sew

Finished pocket from the inside

Sleeve, Shoulder Pad, and Sleeve Head Application

Sew the Sleeve seams and press them open using a sleeve board, seam roll, or rolled-up towel.

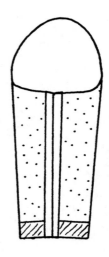

Press the seams open

If you have vents, stitch the seams following the lines of the vents.

Stitch following the line of the vents

Baste the vents closed.

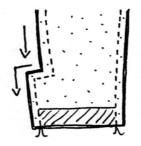

Baste

Clip the seams above the vents so they can be pressed open. Fold the vents toward the Upper Sleeves and baste them at the bottom of the Sleeves.

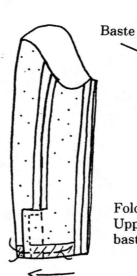

Fold the vents toward Upper Sleeves and baste

Set the Sleeves in the jacket, matching the notches and dots. If you have too much trouble with ease in the sleeve caps, run a gathering stitch between the notches and pull it. Put the eased caps over a sleeve board or ham and steam out the fullness. This should make the Sleeves easier to apply. Trim the entire armhole seams to 1/4". Do not press the seams.

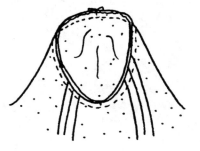

Trim both seams to 1/4"

Good shoulder pads should be narrower at one end than the other, and may have a notch near the centers. Each pad will have a straight edge and a curved edge. The best pads are constructed of densely packed fiber-fill and should have a con- toured shape that conforms to the curve of the shoulders. Try to find ones that resemble the picture as closely as possi- ble because these will not make unsightly bulges.

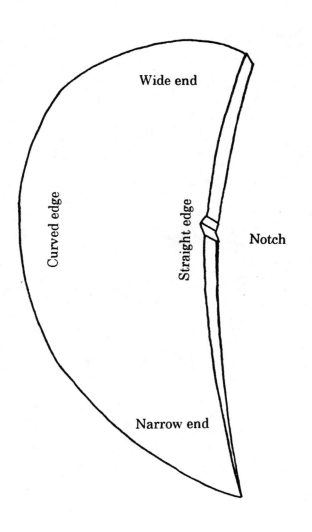

Wide end

Curved edge

Straight edge

Notch

Narrow end

Put the narrow end of the shoulder pad toward the back of the jacket, and the notch at the shoulder seam (if there's no notch, there should be a little more pad toward the back.) Line the straight edge flush with the 1/4" armhole seam, and using the widest and longest zig-zag stitch on your machine, sew the pad to the armhole seam allowance. If you do not have a zig-zag stitch, use two rows of straight stitching. Tack the curved edge of the pad to one side of the shoulder seam with a few machine stitches.

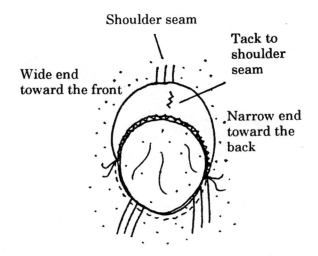

Sleeve heads are used in the armhole seams to give body and smoothness to the sleeve caps. On a 12" head, put a pin at 5 1/2". This marks the position of the shoulder seam. With the longer end of the head to the back of the jacket, zig-zag the head to the armhole seam allowance. The head will extend into the cap of the Sleeve.

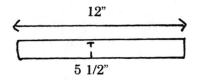

Sleeve Head

When the jacket is turned right side out, the pad will make the seams point out automatically. Now press the sleeve and shoulder over a sleeve board and allow them to cool.

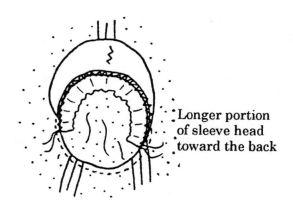

Tacking the Facing

Turn the
Facing back

Use a running stitch
to attach the Facing to the jacket

Fold the Facing back 1" and tack it to the jacket all around using a long, loose, running stitch. The stitches should be invisible on the right side. Lay the jacket flat on a table and start sewing 3" from the bottom edge. Go back and forth from the jacket to the Facing. You can usually connect interfacing to interfacing along the front of the jacket. When tacking in the shoulder and neck areas, put the shoulders inside out over your knee so your sewing path will be more visible and free from wrinkles.

Lining

1. Sew the entire body of the lining together and press the seams open. If there is a CB pleat, sew it together on the machine for 2" at the top and 2" at the bottom, inserting tape into the seam for reinforcement. Leave the waist area free for ease of movement.

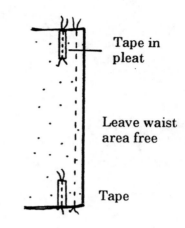

Tape in pleat

Leave waist area free

Tape

If there is a back vent, sew up to it and backstitch. Press the edges under 5/8" around the vent.

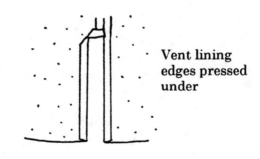

Vent lining edges pressed under

2. Set in the Sleeves. The lining Sleeves will be very hard to ease in, so take two tucks, one on each side of the shoulder dots. This will decrease bulk and make the application easier.

Tucks

3. Trim the armhole seams to 1/4" all around.

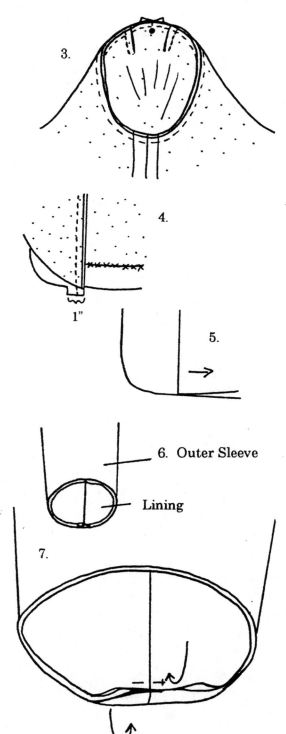

3.

4. Pin the lining to the Facing, right sides together, and sew all around. You may need to clip the lining in the neck area to get it to fit the Back Neck Facing. At the bottom, sew the lining as far as it will go to the 1" of Facing that was left undone.

4.

1"

5. Turn the lining and jacket right sides out and press the seams. Both seams go toward the lining.

5.

6. Pull the Sleeve lining down inside the jacket Sleeve so the two are even. They will be wrong sides together. Line up the lining Sleeve seams with the jacket Sleeve seams so they are face to face.

6. Outer Sleeve

Lining

7.

7. Turn the seams inward toward each other and under 5/8" as if they were sewn together. Secure them with a pin.

8. Go between the jacket and the lining and grasp the seams that are held together by the pin. Remove the pin, but do not let go of the seams!

9. Holding the seams firmly, turn the Sleeve inside out.

10. Begin sewing the two seams together and continue around the Sleeve bottom. When completed, the lining Sleeve and the jacket Sleeve will resemble a tube. The rest of the jacket will look like a twisted mess.

11. Turn the jacket right side out and press the hem up. Both jacket and lining seams go up.

12. Tack the hem down by stitching in the ditch by hand. The ditch is where the lining and the Sleeve are connected. Stitch the ditch just catching the outside of the jacket Sleeve. Use a looped running stitch as described in the illustrations.

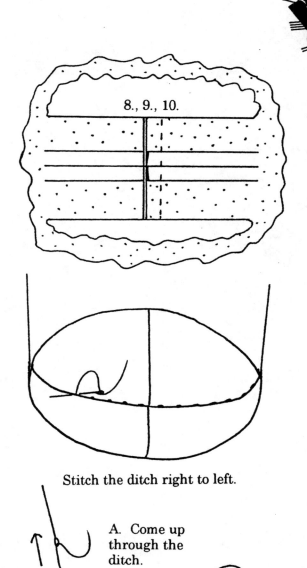

Stitch the ditch right to left.

A. Come up through the ditch.

B. Loop back behind the stitch.

C. Go into the ditch right behind the stitch and come up 1/4" to the left of it.

For vents, sew buttons to the
Sleeves. Position the buttons
1" from the bottom of the Sleeves
and 1/4" from the edge of the
vents. This is not a hard and
fast rule, so personal preference
takes precedence. Remove the
basting threads from the vents.

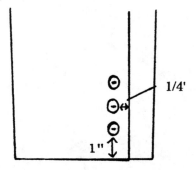

Sew buttons to the Sleeves

13. Lay the jacket open on a table with the lining exposed. Peel back the lining and you will see the lining side seams and the jacket side seams are lying open, face to face. Starting 3" down from the armholes, stitch one side of the lining side seams to one side of the jacket side seams (or side back seams) using a basting stitch on the machine. Stop 3" from the bottom.

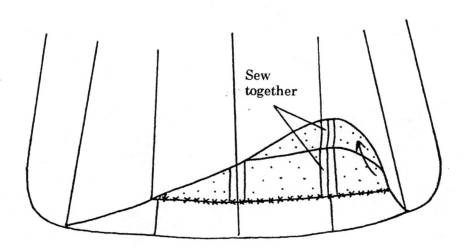

Sew
together

14. Turn the lining hem under and press it. the lining will be flush with the jacket bottom where it is connected to the lower Front Facing, and then it gradually angles up so it is 1/2" from the bottom in the middle.

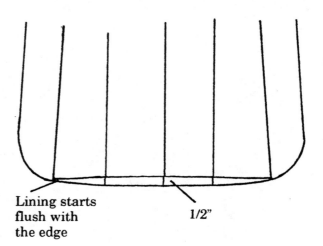

Lining starts
flush with
the edge

1/2"

15. There should be some give or play at the bottom of the lining to allow for ease of movement. To accomplish this, turn the folded lining edge back and stitch 1/4" from it. Go through only one layer of lining fabric. Use a running stitch.

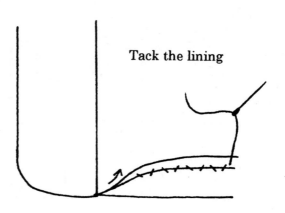

Tack the lining

16. Tack around the vent if there is one. You may want to topstitch the lining to the edge of the vent on the left side.

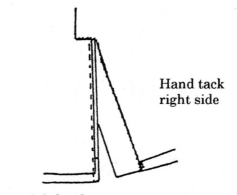

Hand tack
right side

Topstitch left side

Topstitching

Begin stitching at the inside bottom of the right side, about 1/2" into the lining. Stitch up to the lapel, around the collar, and down the other side.

If you are topstitching away from the edge, stitch up to the collar edge, pivot, taking a few stitches in the ditch, and continue around the collar (Fig. A).

If you are topstitching close to the edge, stitch up to the collar, pivot, and continue stitching (Fig. B).

Leave long thread ends at the beginning and end of the stitching line so the outside thread can be pulled through to the inside. Knot the two threads, thread the ends through a needle, and sew between the layers of fabric, hiding the ends. On the first stitch you can pull the knot to the inside like quilters do.

Now apply machine button-holes and sew on buttons.

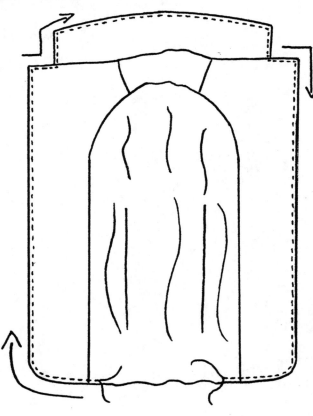

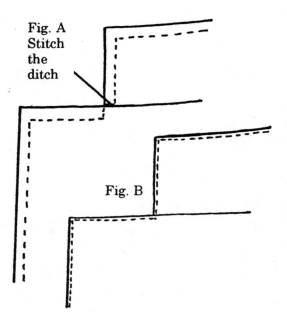

Fig. A
Stitch
the
ditch

Fig. B

Final Pressing and Care

Now that the jacket is complete, we need to do a final press. All the individual parts of the jacket have been pressed, so retouch each area as needed and then press the front, sides, and back.

Go over the collar from the underside and then fold it back. Grasp the fold at the back of the neck and press it hard using a pressing ham to simulate the shape of the neck. Redo the shoulders on a sleeve board or rolled-up towel. If the lapels are not lying back, hold the iron over them and steam them into place. You have probably noticed the absence of twill tape in the collar and lapel roll lines. Fusible interfacing allows us to press and steam the roll lines in place and gives the support needed to hold them there. Lastly, curve the pockets over a ham or rolled towel and press them so they will follow the curves of the body.

From now on, always hang your jacket on a padded or wooden hangar in order to support the shoulders. Before driving in a car, remove the jacket, fold it in half lengthwise, and lay it over the back of the seat. When removing it in public, fold it in the same way and carry it over your arm or drape it over the back of a chair. Always dry-clean your jacket to preserve the valuable tailoring you have done.

Other Publications by Mary Roehr

Pressing to Perfection is the 1-hour companion video to *Speed Tailoring*. Author and tailor, Mary Roehr demonstrates the principles of pressing and the use of fusible interfacing so even beginning seamstresses can succeed in tailoring projects. She discusses pressing equipment, chestpiece and twill tape application, the difference between a hard press and a soft press, how to look taller and thinner by pressing, and much more. See how tailors actually do the final press on a jacket or coat. $24.95

Sewing As A Home Business tells how to start and operate a sewing business in your home. It includes licensing, taxes, advertising, customer relations, target markets, bookkeeping, financing, and insurance. There are complete price lists for custom sewing and alterations for men and women, and discussion on how to figure an hourly rate. If you have a sewing business in your home or have throught about starting one, this book is for you! $14.95

Altering Women's Ready-to-Wear is 200 pages and contains over 300 illustrations. Follow step-by-step directions for altering pants, skirts, blouses, dresses, jackets, coats, and miscellaneous clothing. It discusses fitting, marking, pressing, ironing, steaming, hand sewing, and coping with customer complaints. A complete price list is included as well as a comprehensive index. Whether you want to alter your own clothing or if you do alterations for others, finally all your questions will be answered! $19.95

Altering Men's Ready-to-Wear is 150 pages with hundreds of illustrations. Pictures show how to identify the problem and what to do to correct it. Included are pants, shirts, jackets, coats, vests, and neckties. Marking, pressing, hand sewing, and prices for men's alterations are there too. A handy index will help you locate the solution to your problem quickly. If you have wanted to alter men's clothing, now is the time to start! $17.95

Sew Hilarious is sewing's first cartoon book. Laugh to 64 pages of hilarious cartoons that pertain to all aspects of sewing including learning to sew, sewing equipment and materials, sewing as therapy, sewing getaways, sewing for others, and more. Anyone who sews will see themselves in the last chapter, "The Life of a Fabriholic." This book makes a great gift! $9.95

Speed Tailoring $14.95

For ordering or more information:
Mary Roehr Books & Video, 500 Saddlerock Circle, Sedona, AZ 86336
520-282-4971
Check, Money Order, Visa, Mastercard, Discover, American Express
Please add $2.50 postage for the first item, $1.00 each additional